NORTH AMERICAN NATURAL RESOURCES

FRESHWATER RESOURCES

North American Natural Resources

Coal

Copper

Freshwater Resources

Gold and Silver

Iron

Marine Resources

Natural Gas

Oil

Renewable Energy

Salt

Timber and Forest Products

Uranium

NORTH AMERICAN NATURAL RESOURCES

FRESHWATER RESOURCES

John Perritano

MASON CREST

Mason Crest
450 Parkway Drive, Suite D
Broomall, PA 19008
www.masoncrest.com

MTM Publishing, Inc.
435 West 23rd Street, #8C
New York, NY 10011
www.mtmpublishing.com

President: Valerie Tomaselli
Vice President, Book Development: Hilary Poole
Designer: Annemarie Redmond
Illustrator: Richard Garratt
Copyeditor: Peter Jaskowiak
Editorial Assistant: Andrea St. Aubin

Series ISBN: 978-1-4222-3378-8
ISBN: 978-1-4222-3381-8
Ebook ISBN: 978-1-4222-8555-8

Library of Congress Cataloging-in-Publication Data
Perritano, John.
  Freshwater Resources / by John Perritano.
    pages cm. — (North American natural resources)
  Includes bibliographical references and index.
  ISBN 978-1-4222-3381-8 (hardback)—ISBN 978-1-4222-3378-8 (series)—ISBN 978-
1-4222-8555-8 (ebook)
1. Water supply—Juvenile literature. 2. Water consumption—North America—
Juvenile literature. 3. Hydrological cycle—Juvenile literature. I. Title.
  GB662.3.G365 2015
  333.91—dc23
                              2015005845

Printed and bound in the United States of America.

First printing
9 8 7 6 5 4 3 2 1

TABLE OF CONTENTS

Key Icons to Look for:

Words to Understand: These words with their easy-to-understand definitions will increase the reader's understanding of the text, while building vocabulary skills.

Sidebars: This boxed material within the main text allows readers to build knowledge, gain insights, explore possibilities, and broaden their perspectives by weaving together additional information to provide realistic and holistic perspectives.

Research Projects: Readers are pointed toward areas of further inquiry connected to each chapter. Suggestions are provided for projects that encourage deeper research and analysis.

Text-Dependent Questions: These questions send the reader back to the text for more careful attention to the evidence presented there.

Series Glossary of Key Terms: This back-of-the-book glossary contains terminology used throughout the series. Words found here increase the reader's ability to read and comprehend higher-level books and articles in this field.

Note to Educator: As publishers, we feel it's our role to give young adults the tools they need to thrive in a global society. To encourage a more worldly perspective, this book contains both imperial and metric measurements as well as references to a wider global context. We hope to expose the readers to the most common conversions they will come across outside of North America.

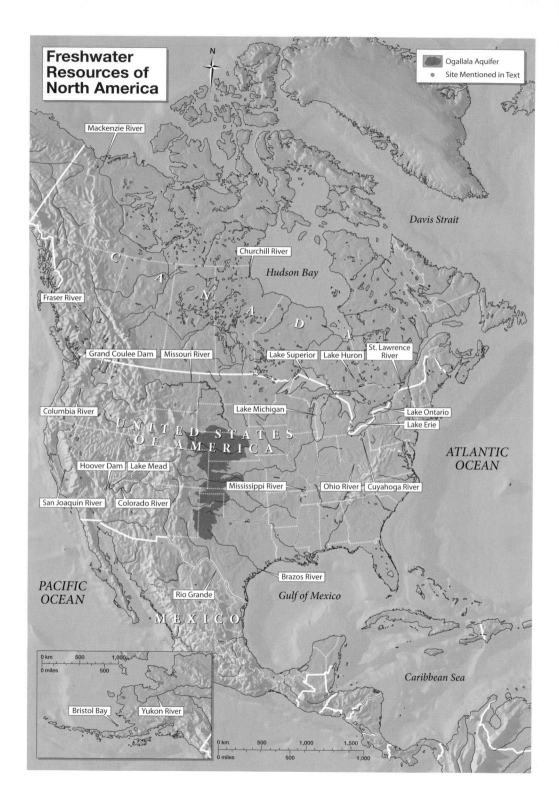

Freshwater Resources of North America

Ogallala Aquifer
Site Mentioned in Text

N

Mackenzie River

Davis Strait

Churchill River

Hudson Bay

Fraser River

C A N A D A

Grand Coulee Dam   Missouri River   Lake Superior   Lake Huron   St. Lawrence River

Columbia River

U N I T E D   S T A T E S
O F   A M E R I C A

Lake Michigan   Lake Ontario
Lake Erie

ATLANTIC
OCEAN

Hoover Dam   Lake Mead

Mississippi River   Ohio River   Cuyahoga River

San Joaquin River   Colorado River

PACIFIC
OCEAN

Brazos River

Rio Grande   Gulf of Mexico

M E X I C O

Caribbean Sea

0 km   500   1,000
0 miles   500

Bristol Bay   Yukon River

0 km   500   1,000   1,500
0 miles   500   1,000

INTRODUCTION

W e brush our teeth with it. We drink it. We use it to wash our cars, our clothes, and ourselves. We cook with it, swim in it, fish in it, wade in it. We need it to grow crops and flush our toilets. Without it, our bodies would wither. It comes out of faucets and

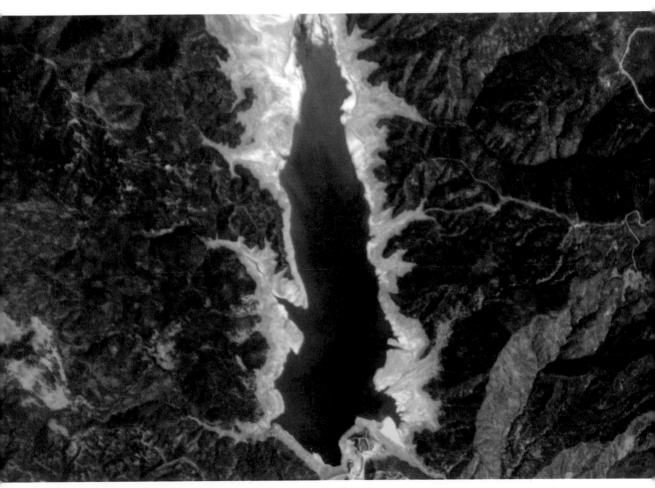

The impact of drought can be seen in this 2014 satellite image of California's Indian Valley Reservoir. In a non-drought year, there would be ten times as much freshwater, covering twice the area shown here. (Planet Labs, Inc./Wikimedia)

puddles on the road. We can put it in a glass, chug it from a bottle, or gulp it from a fountain. We travel under it, over it, and above it.

Water is one of the most vital resources on the planet. It determines where we live and what our quality of life is like. Yet we humans often abuse water. We taint it with chemicals and human sewage. We waste it. As Earth's population continues to grow and the planet warms, there's just not going to be enough freshwater to go around.

Seems strange, doesn't it? After all, if scientists could build a drinking glass as large as the United States and fill it with every drop of water on the planet, the glass would be 90 miles (144.84 kilometers) tall. With all this water, you would think everyone would have enough water to drink.

That's just not the case.

There exists only about 8.4 million cubic miles (35 million cubic kilometers) of usable freshwater on the planet. Freshwater is becoming scarce because of overuse, an ever-increasing population, and climate change. Growing cities, slaking thirsts, energy production, and industrial uses are making water more precious than gold, silver, or crude oil.

Chapter One

THE IMPORTANCE OF WATER

Mark Butler wasn't going anywhere. When a massive storm blew across the Pacific Ocean in early December 2014, Northern California received between 3 and 6 inches (8 to 15 cm) of rainfall, while Southern California got 1 to 3 inches (2 to 8 cm). That might not sound like a lot, but it was nearly double the average annual rainfall expected in the Bay Area.

Words to Understand

aquifers: underground chambers that contain water.

deficit: shortfall or shortage.

hydrologic cycle: events in which water vapor condenses and falls to the surface as rain, snow, or sleet, and then evaporates and returns to the atmosphere.

metabolism: the biological process by which food is converted into energy.

precipitation: rain, hail, or snow.

runoff: water not absorbed by the soil that flows into lakes, streams, rivers, and oceans.

Flooded San Joaquin River delta in northern California, in 2009.

Butler, who lived at the R.C. Mobile Park in Redwood City near San Francisco, watched as the rain fell and the floodwaters raged. Many of his neighbors decided to evacuate. Some left for higher ground, while others stayed with family, friends, or sought help from the Red Cross. Butler wasn't budging, though. He had a dog to take care of. Instead of hightailing it out of there, he sealed the heating vents and other openings in his house with duct tape.

The rain continued to fall, and the floodwaters continued to rise. The water seeped through the tape and came through the walls of Butler's house. When the rains finally ended, Butler's house was completely flooded, "but I can deal with it," he told a reporter. "I'm not going to leave the dog. She has separation anxiety. She's all I got."

Butler wasn't the only one who had to deal with the terrible weather. There was so much water at another trailer park that residents used trash cans to bail floodwaters out of their living rooms. "Water went into my house. My stuff is destroyed," said one woman.

> **Water by the Numbers**
>
> Chemical formula: H_2O
> Phase at room temperature: liquid
> Freezing point: 32°F (0°C)
> Boiling point: 212°F (100°C)

Scientists couldn't believe what was happening. More rain fell in that one week in California then in all of the previous winter. **Runoff** caused water levels to surge and rivers and streams to rise. When the water had nowhere else to go, it flooded roadways and homes, backyards, stores, and neighborhoods. But while the storm was painful and destructive, it was a welcome relief for an area devastated by a massive drought. Droughts are long periods of abnormally low **precipitation** that result in a shortage of water.

Drought is an experience Californians know all too well. From December 1, 2012, to November 29, 2014, San Francisco had a 20.9-inch (53 centimeter) rainfall **deficit**, while Los Angeles had a nearly a 15-inch (38 centimeter) deficit. While the massive

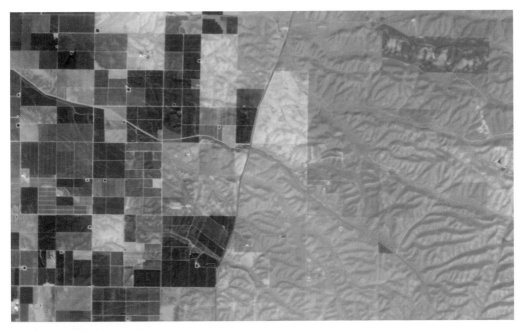

A 2014 satellite image of Bakersfield, California, shows the contrast between agricultural fields, which are watered, and the desert-like surroundings.

storm added much-needed water to the region's reservoirs, much more precipitation was still required to erase the long-term dry spell. That dry spell was so bad in January 2014 that California's governor Jerry Brown declared a drought emergency. He asked all of the state's residents to cut their water use by 20 percent. The drought was so bad that special satellites orbiting 248.55 miles (400 kilometers) above the planet could see that the state's groundwater resources were drying up.

Taking Water for Granted

Most of us take water for granted. After all, we're surrounded by it: two-thirds of the planet is covered by water. But if there's so much water around, why are California and other areas of North America, not to mention the world, so dry?

The answer is simple. While up to 97 percent of the world's water is salt water, which humans can't drink or use, just 3 percent is freshwater, the main ingredient for life. Most of that—about 2 percent—is locked away in the polar ice caps or in underground chambers called **aquifers**. It's hard to get that water out of the ground, so there's only about 8.4 million cubic miles (35 million cubic kilometers) of usable freshwater on the planet.

What does all this mean? All 7 billion of us who live on Earth have to share that 1 useable percent of the world's total water supply. And while we add about 85 million people to the planet each year, Earth is not making any more water. All the moisture that we have on the planet today is all that we will ever have.

Water as Life

When scientists search for life in outer space, they look for evidence of water. Why? Because where there's water, life might exist. Everything on Earth, from the largest whale to the tiniest bacterium, needs water to survive. So when telescopes peer deep into the universe and spaceships orbit or motor around the Martian landscape, they look for evidence of water.

Humans cannot exist without water. Water makes up roughly 60 percent of our bodies. Water dissolves nutrients and vitamins from the food we eat and delivers them

Although they float in the sea, most icebergs are made of freshwater.

to our cells. Our bodies also use water to flush out toxic substances. In the form of sweat, water regulates our body temperature by cooling us when we overheat. Water also helps us our body's **metabolism**, by turning food and oxygen into a form that we can use as energy.

Plants also need water to grow. Most plants are 90 percent water. They need water for photosynthesis, the process by which they produce food. During photosynthesis, plants create glucose, a kind of sugar, from a combination of the sun's light, carbon dioxide and water. Water can cool a plant when the temperature rises. And plants also use water for transportation. Seeds can fall in a river or stream and make their way to a different area where they can take root and grow.

The Water Cycle

When you want a glass of water, it is as easy as turning on the faucet. However, water has to go through several steps before you can fill your glass. Most of the water we drink comes from underground sources or from surface water, such as rivers, lake, and reservoirs. How did the water get there? The answer lies in the **hydrologic cycle**, a series of events that began long before dinosaurs walked the planet.

The hydrologic, or water, cycle is the process by which the sun's energy moves water between the oceans and the sky. Here's how it works: the sun causes moisture to evaporate, which produces water vapor. As the water vapor moves up through the

On Ice

Freshwater in North America is also bound up in hundreds of glaciers. The state of Washington has about 186 named glaciers, while California has 20. These glaciers developed millions of years ago, when layer upon layer of snow compacted over time into thick sheets of ice. A small glacier might be no larger than a football field, while some glaciers can be the size of continents. In many parts of the world, glaciers are an important source of freshwater. In the Himalayan Mountains, for example, melting glaciers provide freshwater for nearly a half-a-billion people living in India, Pakistan, and elsewhere.

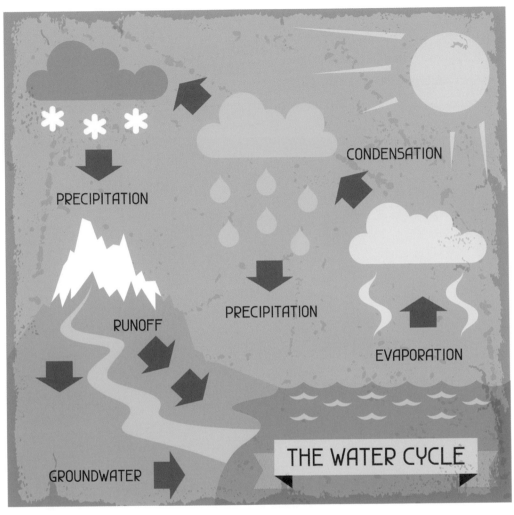

The hydrologic cycle, also called the water cycle.

cool atmosphere, it begins clinging to airborne dust particles, which create clouds. Eventually, the water vapor turns to rain, snow, and other forms of precipitation.

Access to Water

The hydrologic cycle occurs every hour, of every day, of every year. That's a good thing, because we need every drop of water we can get. Without water, life cannot exist. We need water to drink, grow our food, and generate power. Animals need water to live. Yet 1 billion people lack access to clean drinking water.

Part of the reason is that some countries have more water than other countries. In North America, people in the United States and Canada have better access to clean water than those living in Haiti or other Caribbean islands. Moreover, the water that

At Awerial, a settlement for displaced people in South Sudan, a boy shows the difference between water from the river Nile before (left) and after (right) it has been treated and made drinkable.

Where Water Is Found on Earth

Here's where all the water is kept on the planet:

Salt water (oceans): 96.5 percent

Freshwater frozen in glaciers, ice caps, and permanent snow: 1.74 percent

Freshwater trapped underground: 76 percent

Freshwater found on the surface in rivers, lakes, and swamps: 0.0098 percent

people in these countries do find is often not clean enough to drink. Sometimes it's too expensive for these countries to drill wells and tap underground water sources. Many countries cannot afford the price of building dams to create reservoirs, which capture water for use. In some poor countries, women spend up to eight hours a day searching for clean water to use.

The problems associated with the lack of clean water are expected to get worse. A 2012 report by the US Director of National Intelligence warned that the lack of water in certain countries, especially those in the Middle East and Asia, could impact the security of the United States. According to the report, "during the next 10 years, many countries important to the United States will experience water problems—shortages, poor water quality, or floods—that will risk instability and state failure, increase regional tensions, and distract them from working with the United States." The lack of water could threaten food production, energy supplies, and create stress on poor countries.

While there are many reasons why freshwater is in such short supply, they all boil down to three underlying problems: global warming, pollution, and the world's ever-increasing population.

TEXT-DEPENDENT QUESTIONS

1. Describe how the water cycle works.
2. How much of Earth's water is freshwater? How much of that is locked away in the polar ice caps and aquifers?
3. Explain how water evaporates.

RESEARCH PROJECTS

1. Use a rain gauge to collect and measure how much rainfall your community receives in a given week or month. Create a line or bar chart outlining the measurements.
2. Complete this activity to see the water cycle in action: fill a mixing bowl a quarter of the way with water. Put a coffee mug in the center of the mixing bowl. Place plastic wrap over the top of the bowl and secure it with a rubber band or string. Come back in a day or two to see what happens. If you want to speed up the process, put the bowl in a warm place. Record your observations.

Chapter Two

FORMATION AND LOCATION

Understanding the water cycle is important, but it doesn't explain how water first arrived on Earth. It's an amazing story that began some 3.7 billion years ago with the Big Bang. The Big Bang was the mother of all explosions. It sparked the formation of our solar system and the universe itself. From that initial blast, everything in the universe formed—including the stars, the planets, and us.

Words to Understand

aquatic: relating to organisms that live in water.

erosion: gradual wearing away of rock due to wind, water, or ice.

molecules: smallest parts of a chemical compound, consisting of two or more atoms held together by chemical forces.

nuclei: centers of atoms.

porous: able to permit liquid to pass through.

tectonic: relating to the structure and movement of Earth's crust.

tributaries: streams, lakes, and wetlands that drain into a river.

That's because the explosion threw out a massive unformed cloud of particles. The blast had so much energy that within three minutes or so those particles started to cook, break apart, and band together to make larger particles called atomic **nuclei.** Among the nuclei was hydrogen, one of the two main ingredients in water.

Oxygen, the other ingredient, formed about a billion years after the Big Bang. That's when stars began fusing the nuclei from the Big Bang in their superheated

The comet Bradfield photographed over northeastern Colorado in 2004.

cores. As that happened, more complex elements, including carbon, nitrogen, and oxygen formed.

Eventually, many stars began to die as they used up all their hydrogen and helium fuel. As that happened, fusion stopped, and gravity caused the stars to collapse on themselves. Eventually, each star exploded, releasing massive amounts energy and sending out billions of atoms of various elements, including hydrogen and oxygen, into space.

Over time, hydrogen **molecules** combined with oxygen molecules to create H_2O—water. As Earth formed some 4.5 billion years ago, there were water molecules floating around the new planet's interstellar neighborhood. But Earth was too hot and had no atmosphere. The molecules evaporated as they dropped to the planet.

A Collision Course

Over time, however, Earth began to cool. As it did, it was bombarded by comets and asteroids. These hunks of space rocks (especially asteroids), some scientists believe, were the main sources of Earth's water. Comets are dirty snowballs—huge lumps of dirt and rock mixed together with frozen water and many gases. Scientists say after Earth formed, comet after comet and asteroid after asteroid crashed into the planet, depositing a variety of elements and minerals, including those that formed water.

As the centuries ticked by, volcanoes spewed gases, including hydrogen and oxygen, from deep inside the Earth. The gases combined to create water vapor and, eventually, an atmosphere. The water vapor condensed into rain, which fell to the surface. Some of the water fell on land, where it eroded the rocks and picked up minerals like chloride and sodium. This water became the salt water that makes up our oceans.

But some of that precipitation did not end up in the ocean. It became freshwater in lakes, rivers, and streams carved out of Earth's crust by glaciers, **erosion**, or **tectonic** activity. It also soaked into the ground, where it was trapped in underground chambers called aquifers.

Only about 1.2 percent of Earth's surface freshwater is found in rivers, lakes, and wetlands. Land animals, along with many **aquatic** plants and creatures, rely on surface

The Atlantic Ocean and the eastern seaboard of the United States, photographed from space.

water to live. Still, about 30 percent of Earth's freshwater is underground, while nearly 69 percent is locked away in glaciers and the polar ice caps. If you could roll all the fresh liquid water in the ground and on the surface into a sphere, it would form a ball 169.5 miles (272.78 kilometers) in diameter, which would be large enough to cover the state of Kentucky.

The Great Lakes

About 21 percent of the world's supply of fresh surface water is located in North America. In fact, no continent in the world has as much surface water as North America does. Canada alone has at least 3 million freshwater lakes. Moreover, 85 percent of the continent's fresh surface water is located in the Great Lakes of Michigan, Superior, Ontario, Erie, and Huron, which border the United States and Canada.

Sunset over Lake Michigan.

Great Lakes by the Numbers

- The five Great Lakes have a total area of more than 94,000 square miles (almost 25,000 square kilometers). That's larger than the combined land area of New York, New Jersey, Connecticut, Rhode Island, Massachusetts, Vermont, and New Hampshire.
- Only Lake Michigan is entirely within the United States.
- Ninety-five percent of all freshwater in the United States is located in the Great Lakes.
- Ninety-nine percent of the water in the Great Lakes comes from melted glaciers.

These lakes formed around 2 billion years ago, when volcanoes and earthquakes rocked the continent. All that stress created a number of mountain ranges. As these mountains pushed upwards, they created depressions on the

The Great Lakes photographed by space shuttle *Discovery* in 1994. Lake Ontario is in the foreground and Detroit is visible just above the center.

surface. About 2 billion years later, the surrounding seas poured into these depressions, eroding the region even more.

About 2 million or so years ago, massive glaciers inched forward, and then backward, carving out huge slices of land. The weight of all this ice depressed Earth's surface even more. When the glaciers finally retreated, they started to melt, forming large glacial lakes—the Great Lakes. The lakes were much larger then than they are today. Over time, the land began to rise, causing dramatic changes in the size, depth, and drainage patterns of the Great Lakes.

Tunnels of Water

Nearly a third of the freshwater on the planet sits in aquifers. These underground chambers can occur at various depths, and they can be huge or only a few acres wide. The surrounding rock has to be very **porous** so groundwater can travel from the surface down to the aquifer. Rocks, such as sandstone and limestone, along with sand and gravel, make for good aquifers. Most aquifers are not raging underground rivers. That's because water moves slowly through the ground as it squeezes through the rock.

Well water is drawn from aquifers. The wells, along with the aquifer, replenish themselves when water seeps into the ground after it rains or the snow melts.

In the High Plains of the United States sits the Ogallala Aquifer, one of the largest aquifers in the world. Encompassing some 174,000 square miles (about 450,000 square kilometers) in eight states, including South Dakota, Nebraska, Kansas, Colorado, and

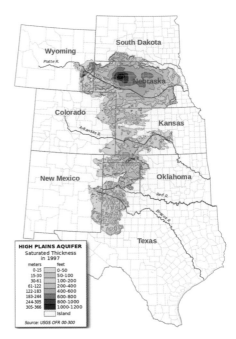

A map of the Ogallala Aquifer. The colors are measurements of "saturated thickness," which is a way of talking about how much water is trapped in the aquifer.

What Happens When It Rains?

When it rains, does it really pour? It depends. The following chart from the US Geological Survey indicates how many gallons of water pour down when 1 inch of rain falls.

Area	Amount of water
Roof of a house (40 x 70 feet)	1,743 gallons
1 acre	27,154 gallons
1 square mile	17.38 million gallons
United States	61,474 billion gallons

Wyoming, the Ogallala is a vast underground reservoir that provides this fertile region with life-sustaining food, including fields of corn, sorghum, soybeans, wheat, and cotton. The Ogallala is about 10 million years old. If you could spread the Ogallala Aquifer across the United States, it would drown all 50 states under 1.5 feet (0.45 meters) of water. The aquifer is so large that if you were able to pump all the water out, it would take 6,000 years to refill naturally.

Like many aquifers, however, the Ogallala is being depleted. Humans are taking water out of the ground faster than the water cycle can replenish it.

Watersheds

Watersheds, sometimes called drainage basins, are areas drained by a river and its **tributaries**. Most of the freshwater that flows on Earth's surface flows through watersheds. Eventually, all this water ends up in the oceans. Such is the case with the Mississippi River watershed—the second largest in the world. The water from the Mississippi watershed empties into the Gulf of Mexico.

North America's Continental Divide is also a vast watershed that follows the ridges of the Rocky Mountain range in Canada and the United States. Precipitation that falls on the west side of the Rockies flows into the Pacific Ocean, while all the rain, snow, and ice that falls on the east side of the mountains flows into the Atlantic and Arctic Oceans.

The Mississippi River.

TEXT-DEPENDENT QUESTIONS

1. Where is most of North America's fresh surface water located?
2. Name the five Great Lakes.
3. How did glaciers form?

RESEARCH PROJECTS

1. Try this experiment to understand how groundwater moves: mix about two cups of sand and two cups of small pebbles or gravel in a bowl. Pour the mixture into a one-quart transparent jar. Pour a half a cup of water into the jar. Put the jar into a warm area and let it sit for three or four days. Observe what happens. Record your results.
2. The Great Lakes are the world's largest bodies (in terms of surface area) of freshwater. Create a chart for each of the five Great Lakes, showing the average depth, volume of water in cubic miles, area (square miles), and deepest points of each lake.

Chapter Three

SCIENCE AND USES

Water is the most important resource we have. It's more important than oil, gold, or iron. Without water, cultures and nations could not exist. Water was so important to our ancestors that the planet's earliest civilizations grew up around rivers. These river valleys had fertile land that provided early farmers with a bounty of crops. In these areas, people built cities. These rivers, such as the Nile in Egypt and the Indus in India, also acted as "highways," allowing people to travel and trade with each other.

Words to Understand

hydroelectric: electricity created by running water.

irrigate: to supply an area with water, especially to grow crops.

turbines: machines in which moving water or steam slams into rotors or blades to produce electricity.

Irrigation machinery used on crops.

Yet, as we've discussed, water is a not an unlimited resource. We humans consume six times as much water as we did only 100 years ago. That's because during the last century, the world's population tripled. That means more cooking, drinking, washing dishes, brushing teeth, and flushing toilets. But water use in the home accounts for only a fraction of the total water we use. Industry uses twice as much water as households—mostly in the production of electricity and food.

The Water Supply

Drinking and cooking are two of the most important uses of water, which is why many states, provinces, towns, and cities in North America take great care in making

Freshwater Use by the Numbers

Used in electric power plants: 41.5 percent
Used for irrigation: 37 percent
Used for domestic household purposes: 8.5 percent
Used by non-households that are hooked up to public water supplies: 5.4 percent
Used in industry: 5 percent
Used in aquaculture, or fish farming: 2.6 percent

sure everyone has enough water. These communities provide residents with drinking water from nearby rivers, lakes, or underground water sources. Some homes, however, rely on water from private wells, while other people buy water from water companies.

Power Generation

Just southeast of Las Vegas, Nevada, in a place called the Black Canyon, sits one of the great technological marvels of the world—the Hoover Dam. Before the dam was built, most of the American Southwest was a dry, inhospitable place that many people

Hydroelectric turbines at the Hoover Dam.

avoided. Then, in 1936, the Hoover Dam changed the course of the Colorado River. Suddenly arid states such as California and Arizona were turning green as farmers **irrigated** their fields. Cities grew. The population exploded.

Built mainly to prevent flooding on the river, the Hoover Dam uses the water of the Colorado River to generate power. The dam, which stands 726 feet (221.28 meters) tall and is 1,244 feet (379.17 meters) long, was at the time one of the largest human-made structures in the world, and one of the planet's largest producers of **hydroelectric** power.

Capturing and using rushing water as a source of power has been going on for centuries. Thousands of years ago, the ancient Greeks made the first waterwheel, which they used to grind wheat into flour and to cut wood to make homes.

These days, hydropower can keep a building cool in the summer or light a streetlamp at night. Dams on rivers produce most of the world's hydroelectricity by using a version of the ancient waterwheel. Rushing water passes through these modern waterwheels, known as **turbines**, which then spin and generate power.

The world's largest hydroelectric plant is the Three Gorges Dam in China. It uses 32 turbines. The Grand Coulee Dam on the Columbia River in Washington State is the largest hydroelectric plant in North America. It has three power plants and is the largest producer of hydroelectric power in the United States, generating enough electricity to power 2.3 million homes for one year.

Hydropower is big business and accounts for nearly 20 percent of the world's power supply. Hydropower is not only the world's largest source of renewable energy, it's also the most efficient. While a typical power plant fueled by oil, natural gas, or coal is able to convert about 50 percent of available energy into electricity, a large-scale hydropower plant converts 90 percent. Still, about two-thirds of the planet's hydropower potential remains untapped. Experts estimate that over the next few decades, hydropower will grow 2.5 to 3 percent per year.

Fishing

Perch, trout, salmon. Walleye, pike, bass. They're fun to catch and tasty to eat. Moreover, they're all freshwater fish. Yet they represent only a few of the nearly 800

A girl and her speckled and rainbow trout.

Where Does Water Go?

An average household uses more than 300 gallons (about 1100 liters) of water per day. Outdoor water use accounts for 30 percent of all household use, while 70 percent is used indoors. Where does the water go? Household water use breaks down this way:

- Flushing the toilet: 26.7 percent
- Washing clothes: 21.7 percent
- Turning on the faucet: 15.7 percent
- Taking a shower: 16.8 percent
- Wasted due to leaky pipes: 13.7 percent

fish species that live in the freshwater of North America. Most freshwater fish aren't sport fish. Ninety-five percent of all the freshwater species in the North America are little-known fish such as shiners and darters.

Commercial and freshwater sport fishing are important economic and cultural traditions in North America. In 2013, 28,239 tons of freshwater fish were caught by commercial anglers in Canada, bringing in a total of $60.7 million. On average, each person in Canada consumes nearly a pound of freshwater fish a year.

In the United States, the sport fishing industry supports more than 800,000 jobs, including restaurant and hotel workers, and people who sell fishing tackle, bait, boats, and more. As many as 33 million people, aged 16 or older, go fishing, mostly on freshwater lakes and rivers. They spend about $48 million a year on equipment, licenses, and fishing gear. In 2011, 27 million anglers fished the freshwater resources of United States.

Industrial Uses

Industry needs freshwater, too. Waterways such as the Mississippi River and the Great Lakes are instrumental in transporting goods from one place to the next. Factories need water to process products, clean machinery, and cool buildings and equipment. The steel, chemical, and paper industries all depend on water, as do petroleum refineries. Many industries recycle water and use it over again.

In 2005 (the last time such numbers were available) the mining industry used an estimated 410 billion gallons of water per day. Most of that—57 percent—was in the form of freshwater. Iron ore mining operations in Michigan and Minnesota used the most surface freshwater.

How Much Water Do You Use?

How much water you use per day depends largely on where you live. If you live in Nevada, Idaho, Utah, and Wyoming, you use around 151–200 gallons (about 40 to 50 liters) a day. If you live in Rhode Island, Connecticut, Vermont, New Hampshire, and Maine, you use up to 75 gallons a day.

Scientists survey the quality of water in a mine filtration pond in Pennsylvania. Mining operations have used water for centuries to remove minerals from rock. They use water in the milling (crushing, screening, and washing) of rocks and ore.

TEXT-DEPENDENT QUESTIONS

1. Explain the process of photosynthesis.
2. What is the significance of fishing to Canadian and US economies?
3. Name three industrial uses for water.

RESEARCH PROJECTS

1. Research and write a report that describes where people in your community get the majority of their freshwater. As you conduct your research, answer these questions: What are the sources of this freshwater? How does the water get to individual homes and businesses? Who uses the most water in your community?
2. Do water molecules move faster in hot water than in cold? Try this experiment to find out: Fill a clear glass with hot water. Fill another with cold water. Make sure each glass has the same amount of water. Put a drop of food coloring into both glasses. Watch what happens. What can you conclude?

Chapter Four

ENVIRONMENT

I n the fall of 2014, officials from water agencies in Arizona, California, and Nevada got together to battle one of the greatest problems facing the American Southwest—the lack of water.

The American Southwest is one of the driest places in North America. Although the Hoover Dam helped green these areas decades ago, these days, the region's rivers and lakes are drying up. Every year that there's less snowmelt in the mountains and not enough rainfall, there is less usable freshwater.

Words to Understand

burgeoning: developing quickly.

ecosystems: specific environments with communities of organisms that depend on each other.

greenhouse gases: gases such as carbon dioxide that trap the sun's radiation close to Earth's surface, keeping the planet warm, much like the inside of a greenhouse.

latitudes: imaginary east-west lines around Earth's surface, parallel to the equator.

solvents: substances that can dissolve other substances.

Millions of people in the Southwest get their water from the Colorado River. The river feeds Lake Mead and Lake Powell, which is the main water supply for 22 million people. Farmers use the river to irrigate crops. Factories use the river to make products. People water their lawns and wash their cars from water supplied by the Colorado River.

However, a withering drought has baked the region since 1999. The drought got so bad in 2010 that Lake Mead sank to its lowest level in 75 years. And the problem

Lake Mead stretches across the states of Nevada and Arizona.

is not expected to get better anytime soon. Experts say the Colorado River basin will become increasingly drier as the years pass. Scientists say the region's **burgeoning** population, coupled with climate change, is to blame. Climate change is resulting in an overall rise in Earth's surface temperature. Experts say this trend, along with an increase in water use, will make the Southwest even more parched.

Faced with these problems, water officials in the region agreed in 2014 to add as much as 3 million acres of water to Lake Mead by 2020. How will they do this if there is so little rainfall? They hope to convince residents to conserve water and change the way water resources are managed. If they are successful, they will add about 30 feet (about 9 meters) to Lake Mead. That's about as much water as 6 million homes use in a year.

The Impact of Climate Change

Many scientists say climate change is producing extreme weather conditions that affect our supply of freshwater. Climate change occurs because there are too many **greenhouse gases**, such as carbon dioxide, in Earth's atmosphere. These gases, produced by the burning of fossil fuels such as coal and oil, trap the sun's heat near Earth's surface. When that happens, Earth's surface temperature increases.

This increase in temperature disrupts the water cycle, which is a delicate balance between evaporation and precipitation. The hotter it gets, the more water evaporates. The rate of evaporation affects different parts of the world in different ways. Some areas, such as in Mexico and the American Southwest, dry out, while other areas experience heavy rainfall. In Great Britain, for example, storm after Atlantic storm has overwhelmed the country in recent years. Scientists say that countries in northern **latitudes** and the tropics are getting wetter as countries in middle latitudes are becoming drier.

The impacts can sometimes be devastating. A severe drought in Mexico in 2014 reduced that country's agricultural production by 40 percent, creating food shortages and higher prices for commodities such as corn. The drought ravaged many communities, disrupting the livelihoods of thousands, forcing people to flee to already overcrowded cities.

The impact of drought on Sonoran Desert, Mexico.

The Pollution Connection

Pollution also makes water unsafe. Pollution occurs when poisonous substances are released into the environment. Water pollution can happen naturally, such as when plants decay in a pond, or when natural disasters, such as earthquakes, hurricanes, and tsunamis sweep vast amounts of salt water into freshwater lakes and rivers.

Humans, however, are mostly responsible for pollution. Humans have been dumping hazardous chemicals, raw sewage, and other toxins into the environment for thousands of years. The streets of ancient Rome, for example, were often filled with human sewage, which eventually made its way to the Tiber River, causing a variety of diseases. During the hot summer of 1858, overflowing sewage made the Thames River in London smell so bad that it was called the "Great Stink."

Long ago, nature was able to break down all this waste into less harmful substances. However, as the population grew, water pollution increased. People built

Before stricter environmental protections were in place, polluted rivers were a common sight. Here, low tide revealed barrels that had been dumped into the Snohomish River in Washington in the 1970s.

cities and factories, creating rivers of pollution and mountains of garbage. People needed some place to put all this waste, so they dumped it in waterways, buried it underground, or tossed it into the streets.

All this pollution was too much for nature to handle. The waste ruined rivers and lakes and seeped into the ground, fouling aquifers. Over time, the pollution threw entire **ecosystems** out of balance, killing many species of plants and animals and endangering peoples' lives.

Many things can pollute water. Chemicals are among the largest sources of pollution. Pesticides, fertilizer, household cleaners, and other substances contain chemicals. Rain and snowmelt can carry these poisons into local waterways. Chemical spills can drain into rivers and streams. Even old medicines flushed down the toilet can cause pollution. Scientists say more than a million different chemicals have entered the world's water supplies over the years. Chemical and industrial pollution was so bad in Cleveland, Ohio, that the city's Cuyahoga River caught fire in 1969.

Waste. Animal and human waste can foul water, too. Waste from humans, pets, and livestock contain disease-carrying bacteria that can get into the water supply. In developed countries, water treatment plants are built to clean wastewater. But in poorer countries, these plants are often too expensive to construct, which is one of the reasons waterborne diseases cause four-fifths of all illnesses in poor countries.

In Haiti, 7 out of 10 people do not have clean water to drink, because human sewage contaminates their sources of drinking water. The water becomes polluted because people dump untreated human waste into rivers and streams. They lack

Deadly Water

An estimated 3.3 million people die from water-related health problems every year around the world. Most of those that die are children under age five. That's because they lack access to clean drinking water. More than one-third of the world's population has no access to sanitation facilities. Half of the world's hospital beds are occupied by patients suffering from waterborne diseases. In developing countries, about 80 percent of illnesses are linked to poor water and sanitation conditions.

Untreated sewage flows into Lake Guiaba, near Porto Alegre, Brazil.

running water or a way to purify wastewater, such as a sewage treatment plant. The sewage brims with bacteria. Because no clean alternatives are available, people use water from these dirty waterways for drinking, cooking, and bathing. Moreover, a massive earthquake in 2010 damaged wells and water pipes in Haiti, making clean water even scarcer. Clean water is so rare in Haiti that many children and adults must walk miles to find water to drink.

Acid Rain. Acid rain forms when factories burn fossil fuels, which release sulfur dioxide and nitrogen oxide into the air. These compounds mix with water vapor in

DDT

Perhaps the most infamous insecticide is DDT, which is the abbreviation for dichlorodiphenyltrichloroethane. The Swiss chemist Paul Muller first discovered in DDT in 1939, and it was used with much success during World War II (1939–1945) to kill the mosquitos and other insects that carry dangerous diseases such as malaria and typhus. From 1942 to 1972, an estimated 675,000 tons of DDT was used in the United States, with terrible consequences. The widespread use of DDT was highly toxic to fish and birds. Problems caused by DDT inspired the writing of *Silent Spring* (1962), one of the most famous books of the environmental movement. The United States and Canada banned DDT in the 1970s, but the pesticide is still sometimes used in Mexico.

the atmosphere, creating deadly acids. The acids fall to the ground as a poisonous rain that can harm lakes, streams, and rivers, killing animals and plants.

Acid rain does not stop at a country's border. It became a political issue between Canada and the United States in the 1980s. At the time, Canada complained that pollution from factories and power plants in the United States were fouling its forests and lakes. Since then, the countries enacted rules and regulations that have done a lot to reduce sulfur and nitrogen emissions.

Heavy Metals. Heavy metals, such as arsenic, cadmium, lead, and mercury, are also major contaminants. Industries use these metals for a variety of purposes. When dumped into the environment, these substances are can find their way into freshwater sources, where they accumulate in the tissue of fish and plants.

One infamous case of groundwater contamination occurred in the 1970s, when investigators in Massachusetts discovered that two municipal wells in the city of Woburn were contaminated with industrial **solvents**. Scientists showed that the tainted water was responsible for elevated rates of disease in one neighborhood.

Fertilizers and Pesticides. The fertilizers and pesticides that people use to grow and process food, keep lawns green, and kill unwanted pests are another source of danger. These chemicals run off into lakes, river, streams, and ponds. Once in the

Runoff from farms can carry both soil and chemicals into freshwater sources.

environment, they find their way into the food chain, where they can harm plants, birds, humans, and other wildlife.

Thermal Pollution. Factories and power plants dump hot wastewater into rivers, lakes, and streams. Dumping warm water into sources of freshwater makes it difficult for fish to breathe. That means fish and other aquatic wildlife can suffocate.

Sediments. Sediments can destroy a freshwater ecosystem, too. When too much dirt runs off into the water, fish cannot breathe because the soil clogs their gills. Sediments also make water cloudy, cutting down on the sunlight that aquatic plants need to live. In fact, sediments are such a problem that the Environmental Protection Agency (EPA) has named them the leading cause of surface water pollution.

The Dust Bowl

In the 1930s, desertification wreaked havoc on the Great Plains, turning the region into what historians call the "Dust Bowl." Bad farming practices combined with a severe drought turned many states, including Oklahoma, into dry wastelands. Crops failed. Rivers dried up. Millions of people left their homes to find a better life somewhere else. Since then, however, better farming practices and irrigation methods have prevented the disaster from happening again.

A young boy in the middle of a dust storm, Cimarron County, Oklahoma, 1932.

Desertification

The lack of freshwater is turning some areas in North America into deserts. Many parts of Canada, Mexico, and the United States have become extremely arid over the past several years. In fact, 40 percent of North America's cropland and rangeland has turned to desert. It's a process known as desertification. A healthy arid or semi-arid environment is generally populated by only the small number of animal and plant species that can survive there. As desertification takes place, it dries up much needed farmland.

While desertification can be caused by a changing climate, people are mostly to blame. In general, desertification is caused by diverting rivers and drawing down underground water sources. Desertification is also caused by the overcultivation of land for food production. The problem becomes worse as the population grows.

TEXT-DEPENDENT QUESTIONS

1. Which river is the main water supply for millions of people in the American Southwest?
2. How do insecticides and pesticides affect water quality?
3. How much cropland and rangeland have turned to desert in North America?

RESEARCH PROJECTS

1. Find out about the water quality in your community by talking to experts at a local museum, water department, school, or university. Identify which bodies of water are polluted and why they are polluted. Write a report about your investigation.
2. Go around your community and take pictures of pollution near local waterways. Create a computer slideshow for your class. Write captions for each of the photos you use.

Chapter Five

PROTECTION

Because the amount of usable freshwater is limited, protecting lakes, rivers, watersheds, and underground sources of freshwater has become a major issue. Protecting freshwater resources comes in many forms, including actions taken by civic and conservation groups, governments, and local communities.

Words to Understand

conservationists: advocates for the preservation of the natural world.

environmentalists: people working to protect the environment.

indigenous: native to a specific area.

parliament: the legislative body of several nations, including Canada and Great Britain.

spawn: the laying of fish eggs.

tundra: a treeless plain that has permanently frozen subsoil.

Fishing for sockeye salmon in Bristol Bay.

Such is the case in Bristol Bay, Alaska, where many people are trying to stop a mining company from polluting the watershed. Bristol Bay is a vast wilderness that covers 40,000 square miles that includes **tundra**, wetlands, rivers, and lakes. The rivers and streams that make up the bay's watershed are a sport fisherman's paradise. Anglers from all over the world travel to the Nushagak, Mulchatna, Koktuli, and Kvichak Rivers to catch trophy-sized fish.

It is here, among the moose, sea otters, porcupines, river otters, and wolves that nearly 40 million sockeye salmon return each year to **spawn**. The bay is home to the world's largest run of sockeye salmon. Huge chinook, or king, salmon also populate the watershed, along with rainbow trout.

For thousands of years Bristol Bay has been home to a number of Native American groups that consume the resources of the bay. Sport and commercial fishing are the lifeblood of many of these communities.

Since the early 2000s, the Bristol Bay ecosystem has been at the center of a huge controversy, because a mining company wants to dig a massive gold and copper mine in the region. If built, it would be the largest open pit mine in North America. Miners dig open-pit mines when they find minerals near Earth's surface. They carve the mines out of the rock in vertical sections called benches that resemble a series of steps. Trucks then haul away the debris so workers can use special techniques to separate the gold and copper from rocks and ore. Open-pit mining is the preferred way of mining for gold and copper.

Environmentalists fear that the mine, known as the Pebble Mine, will damage streams, ponds, and wetlands with billions of tons of tailings. Tailings are the waste product left over after the ore containing the gold and copper has been mined. Tailings are a mixture of water, heavy metals, chemical compounds, and other contaminants found in the crushed rock and ore. The plan for Bristol Bay is to create enormous huge tailing dams to hold back the waste. The dams will be taller than the massive Three Gorges Dam in China, which is 600 feet (185 meters) high.

The mine, some people say, will destroy the freshwater the sockeye need to survive. It is in these streams and rivers that the salmon lay their eggs. When the fish hatch, they thrive in the freshwater before heading out to sea.

What Can You Do?

There's no one solution to protecting our water resources. Laws, regulations, and desalination plants are just some of the answers. Conservation can save some water. And you can do a lot, too.

- Do not let water run when you are brushing your teeth.
- Take short showers.
- Fix leaking faucets.
- Do not let the garden hose run when you are watering the lawn or washing the family car.
- Run the dishwasher and clothes washer only when they are full.
- When washing dishes by hand, don't let the water run.
- Don't let tap water run to cool it off. Instead, keep a bottle of water in the refrigerator.
- Plant drought-resistant plants in your yard.
- Don't clean your driveway with a hose and water.

Whatever you can do to conserve water, do it. There's not a lot of it to go around.

Water Woes

Why do some areas have more water than other areas? In some areas, water is physically scarce. In other words, demand outstrips the ability to produce water. The Colorado River basin is a good example of physical scarcity: the river is being overused, creating problems downstream in states such as Arizona.

In other areas, water is scarce because of the unequal distribution of water resources due to "economic scarcity." The Water Project, a group that seeks to help people in Africa find water, argues that some governments, such as those in sub-Saharan Africa, "lack the compassion and good governance" to provide people with an adequate source of water. In many cases, these governments refuse to fund water projects because of political and ethnic conflicts.

The mining company says the economic benefits of Pebble Mine would be great. Construction would create 16,000 jobs, including 5,000 in Alaska alone. The mine would also provide Alaska with $136 to $180 million in taxes and other economic benefits each year.

Bristol Bay is not the only watershed that people are concerned about. Hundreds of watersheds and thousands of freshwater sources in North America are put at risk by human activities. In Canada, the Peel River watershed high in Yukon Province is threatened by the mining industry. For more than three decades, the **indigenous** residents of the region, along with **conservationists**, worked with the government to develop a plan to protect 80 percent of the watershed. In 2011, however, the Yukon government scraped the plan in favor of another that is friendlier to the mining companies.

Laws and Regulations

Keeping water safe is a paramount concern for all communities, which is why every country in North America has developed standards for clean water. For example, a generation ago, many rivers, lakes, streams, and watersheds in the United States were treated as open sewers. People routinely dumped biological and industrial waste directly into these water sources. The quality of water in the United States was so poor that lawmakers had to pass a special law to protect the environment.

That law, the Clean Water Act, was passed in 1972 by the US Congress. The act's goal was to eliminate pollution from the nation's waterways by giving states, cities, counties, and towns money to build sewage treatment plants. The law also established guidelines to reduce the destruction of wetlands. The Clean Water Act also gave the US Environmental Protection Agency the authority to set up quality standards for wastewater and drinking water. And it made it a crime for people to dump toxic substances into American waters. Most of the rivers and lakes in the United States now meet federal safety standards.

Aerial photo of the western Canadian Arctic. Spring has arrived and the ice is beginning to retreat.

The US government has also passed laws specific to many lakes, rivers, and watersheds. For example, the Great Lakes Water Quality Agreement of 1978, signed by the United States and Canada, reduces certain pollutants flowing into the Great Lakes.

Like the United States, Canada and Mexico have their own water-quality laws and standards. The Canadian federal government, for example, uses the Canadian Environmental Protection Act to force corporations to conduct environmental assessment studies for any new project. The Arctic Waters Pollution Prevention Act was passed by the Canadian **parliament** of in 1970 to protect the Arctic waters close to the Canadian border.

Mexico's No. 1 Resource

Mexico also takes the quality of its water seriously. In 1992, the Mexican government passed the National Water Law, which gave the government the power to regulate wastewater discharges. Moreover, in 1989 the Mexican government created the

Oaxaca, Mexico, does not have piped-in water; instead, water is brought in by truck and stored in home tanks.

Desalination Made Simple

A desalination plant sucks up millions of gallons of seawater a day through intake pipes.

Filters remove any sediment, bacteria, and viruses from the water. The seawater is then pumped through a series of filters that remove the salt. The freshwater is then purified, stored, and delivered. The process produces wastewater that is saltier than seawater. Before the wastewater is returned to the ocean, therefore, workers mix the wastewater with less salty seawater to reduce the wastewater's salinity.

National Water Commission to protect the country's dwindling water supply. The commission tries to make sure that Mexican farmers have an adequate source of water and that everyone has access to clean water and proper wastewater treatment facilities. The commission also protects Mexico's aquifers and drainage basins.

The commission has made tremendous strides. In 2007, 90 percent of all Mexicans had access to clean drinking water, a 10 percent increase since the creation of the commission. In the cities, 95 percent of the population has access to clean water, as do 71 percent of those living in rural areas.

Desalination

To increase the amount of freshwater, many countries, including the United States and Mexico, use technology to remove the salt from seawater. It's a process called desalination.

In 2014, a Mexican company and water officials in San Diego County, California, pushed ahead with plans to build a desalination plant in Mexico to pipe freshwater to the United States. The plant was expected to convert up to 100 million gallons of seawater a day. A desalination plant in Baja, a state in Mexico, produces 5.7 million gallons of water a day.

In water-starved California, officials have been talking for years about dipping into the Pacific Ocean to produce much-needed drinking water. As of 2014, 15 projects were moving forward. In fact, the largest ocean desalination plant in the United States is scheduled to open in 2016 near Carlsbad, California.

TEXT-DEPENDENT QUESTIONS

1. Why is there a controversy over Bristol Bay?
2. What is desalination?
3. What law was passed by the US Congress in 1972 to clean up America's waterways? Name a few powers the law gave the government.

RESEARCH PROJECTS

1. Research the cleanup of a waterway, such as Lake Erie, and describe in a written report how the resource was cleaned and what is being done now to make protect it.
2. Create a poster that shows how people can conserve water at home and in school.

Further Reading

BOOKS

Childs, Craig. *The Secret Knowledge of Water: Discovering the Essence of the American Desert*. Boston: Back Bay Books, 2001.

MacQuitty, Miranda. *Ocean*. DK Eyewitness Books. New York: DK Publishing, 2014.

Nadeau, Isaac. *Water in Plants and Animals*. The Water Cycle. New York: PowerKids Press, 2003.

Park, Linda Sue. *A Long Walk to Water: Based on a True Story*. Boston: Sandpiper, 2011.

Taylor-Butler, Christine. *Hydrology: The Study of Water*. True Books: Earth Science. New York: Scholastic, 2012.

ONLINE

Eartheasy: Solutions for Sustainable Living. "25 Ways to Conserve Water in the Home and Yard." http://eartheasy.com/live_water_saving.htm.

Environment Canada. http://www.ec.gc.ca/default.asp?lang=en&n=FD9B0E51-1.

National Geographic. "Water Conservation Tips." http://environment.nationalgeographic.com/environment/freshwater/water-conservation-tips/.

US Environmental Protection Agency. http://www.epa.gov/.

US Geological Survey. "Water Basics." http://water.usgs.gov/edu/mwater.html.

Series Glossary

alloy: mixture of two or more metals.

alluvial: relating to soil that is deposited by running water.

aquicludes: layers of rocks through which groundwater cannot flow.

aquifer: an underground water source.

archeologists: scientists who study ancient cultures by examining their material remains, such as buildings, tools, and other artifacts.

biodegradable: the process by which bacteria and organisms naturally break down a substance.

biodiversity: the variety of life; all the living things in an area, or on Earth on the whole.

by-product: a substance or material that is not the main desired product of a process but happens to be made along the way.

carbon: a pure chemical substance or element, symbol C, found in great amounts in living and once-living things.

catalyst: a substance that speeds up a chemical change or reaction that would otherwise happen slowly, if at all.

commodity: an item that is bought and sold.

compound: two or more elements chemically bound together.

constituent: ingredient; one of the parts of a whole.

contaminated: polluted with harmful substances.

convection: circular motion of a liquid or gas resulting from temperature differences.

corrosion: the slow destruction of metal by various chemical processes.

dredge: a machine that can remove material from under water.

emissions: substances given off by burning or similar chemical changes.

excavator: a machine, usually with one or more toothed wheels or buckets that digs material out of the ground.

flue gases: gases produced by burning and other processes that come out of flues, stacks, chimneys, and similar outlets.

forges: makes or shapes metal by heating it in furnaces or beating or hammering it.

fossil fuels: sources of fuel, such as oil and coal, that contain carbon and come from the decomposed remains of prehistoric plants and animals.

fracking: shorthand for hydraulic fracturing, a method of extracting gas and oil from rocks.

fusion: energy generated by joining two or more atoms.

geologists: scientists who study Earth's structure or that of another planet.

greenhouse gas: a gas that helps to trap and hold heat—much like the panes of glass in a greenhouse.

hydrocarbon: a substance containing only the pure chemical substances, or elements, carbon and hydrogen.

hydrologic cycle: events in which water vapor condenses and falls to the surface as rain, snow, or sleet, and then evaporates and returns to the atmosphere.

indigenous: growing or living naturally in a particular region or environment.

inorganic: compound of minerals rather than living material.

kerogens: a variety of substances formed when once-living things decayed and broke down, on the way to becoming natural gas or oil.

leachate: liquid containing wastes.

mineralogists: scientists who study minerals and how to classify, locate, and distinguish them.

nonrenewable resources: natural resources that are not replenished over time; these exist in fixed, limited supplies.

ore: naturally occurring mineral from which metal can be extracted.

ozone: a form of oxygen containing three atoms of oxygen in a molecule.

porous: allowing a liquid to seep or soak through small holes and channels.

primordial: existing at the beginning of time.

producer gas: a gas created ("produced") by industrial rather than natural means.

reclamation: returning something to its former state.

reducing agent: a substance that decreases another substance in a chemical reaction.

refine: to make something purer, or separate it into its various parts.

remote sensing: detecting and gathering information from a distance, for example, when satellites in space measure air and ground temperature below.

renewable: a substance that can be made, or a process used, again and again.

reserves: amounts in store, which can be used in the future.

runoff: water not absorbed by the soil that flows into lakes, streams, rivers, and oceans.

seismology: the study of waves, as vibrations or "shaking," that pass through the Earth's rocks, soils, and other structures.

sequestration: storing or taking something to keep it for a time.

shaft: a vertical passage that gives miners access to mine.

sluice: artificial water channel that is controlled by a value or gate.

slurry: a mixture of water and a solid that can't be dissolved.

smelting: the act of separating metal from rock by melting it at high temperatures

subsidence: the sinking down of land resulting from natural shifts or human activities.

sustainable: able to carry on for a very long time, at least the foreseeable future.

synthesis: making or producing something by adding substances together.

tailing: the waste product left over after ore has been extracted from rock.

tectonic: relating to the structure and movement of the earth's crust.

watercourse: a channel along which water flows, such as a brook, creek, or river.

Index

About the Author

John Perritano is an award-winning journalist, writer, and editor from Southbury, Connecticut. He has written numerous articles and books on history, culture, and science for publishers that include National Geographic's Reading Expedition Series and its Global Issues Series. He has also contributed to Discovery.com, *Popular Mechanics,* and other magazines and Web sites. He holds a master's degree in American history from Western Connecticut State University.

Photo Credits

Cover

Clockwise from left: iStock.com/Gordo25; iStock.com/sezer66; iStock.com/Dean_Fikar; Dollar Photo Club/chasingmoments; Dollar Photo Club/Deyan Georgiev; iStock.com/crisod; iStock.com/greenicetea.

Interior

Dollar Photo Club: 13 Sergey Shlyaev; 15 incomible; 27 Vladimir Melnikov; 30 Cecilia Lim; 31 tomalu; 34 unclepodger; 38 oneinchpunch; 44 Henrik Larsson.

iStock.com: 33 DawnPoland.

Library of Congress: 46 Arthur Rothstein.

NASA: 22; 24.

Wikimedia Commons: 50 Härmägeddon; 45 Bob Nichols; 10 Doc Searls; 41 Doug Wilson; 23 Ian Rastall; 53 Jeff Schmaltz; 25 Kbh3rd; 45 Lynn Betts; 54 Nsaum75; 16 Oxfam East Africa; 43 Paulo Rsmenezes; 11 Planet Lab Inc.; 20 TheStarmon; 40 Tomas Castelazo.